FROM SEA to SHINING SEA

VERMONT

JAN M. CZECH

Consultants

MELISSA N. MATUSEVICH, PH.D.
Curriculum and Instruction Specialist
Blacksburg, Virginia

CAROL CHATFIELD
Youth Services Librarian
Ilsley Public Library
Middlebury, Vermont

BETH CURTIS
Teaching Librarian
Fairfield Center School
Fairfield, Vermont

CHILDREN'S PRESS®

AN IMPRINT OF SCHOLASTIC INC.

New York • Toronto • London • Auckland • Sydney • Mexico City
New Delhi • Hong Kong • Danbury, Connecticut

Vermont is in the northeastern part of the United States. It is bordered by New York, New Hampshire, Massachusetts, and Canada.

The front cover photo shows a winter scene in Bradford, Vermont.

Project Editor: Meredith DeSousa
Art Director: Marie O'Neill
Photo Researcher: Marybeth Kavanagh
Design: Robin West, Ox and Company, Inc.
Page 6 map and recipe art: Susan Hunt Yule
All other maps: XNR Productions, Inc.

Library of Congress Cataloging-in-Publication Data

Czech, Jan M.
      Vermont / by Jan M. Czech.
          p. cm.—(From sea to shining sea)
          Includes bibliographical references and index.
      ISBN-13: 978-0-531-20816-8
      ISBN-10: 0-531-20816-8

1. Vermont--Juvenile literature. I. Title. II. Series.
F49.3 .C94 2008
974.3—dc22   2007047602

TABLE of CONTENTS

CHAPTER ONE

INTRODUCING THE GREEN MOUNTAIN STATE

In many parts of Vermont, cows and people share the same territory. A kayaker and curious cows meet at Lewis Creek.

Vermont is located in a region called New England, a group of six states (Maine, Vermont, Connecticut, New Hampshire, Rhode Island, and Massachusetts) in the northeastern part of the United States. Although Vermont is one of the largest New England states—it is second in size only to Maine—it is small compared to other states.

However small, Vermont has a lot to offer. Its natural resources make it the perfect place for outdoor activities. It is known for its plentiful ski areas, beautiful fall foliage, miles of hiking trails, and quaint villages.

Skiing means mountains, which can be found almost anywhere in Vermont. Its nickname is the Green Mountain State, after the mountains running down the middle of Vermont. Their name comes from the French words *les monts verts*, which means "green mountains."

The Green Mountain State has a rich history that is reflected in its state motto, "Freedom and Unity." Vermont wasn't always a state. At one time it was a small republic. It printed its own money, had its own postal service, and was independent for more than thirteen years. When it became a state in 1791, Vermont was the first to join the original thirteen states that made up the newly formed United States.

Agriculture has always been an important way of life in Vermont. Dairying is its primary farm industry. Vermont produces more milk than any other New England state. More maple sugar and maple syrup are made in Vermont than in any other state in the country.

What comes to mind when you think of Vermont?

- Freedom fighters during the American Revolution
- Vermonters tapping trees for sap to make maple syrup
- Skiers racing down snow-covered slopes
- Ben and Jerry's Ice Cream Factory churning out delicious flavors
- United States presidents Calvin Coolidge and Chester A. Arthur born and raised in Vermont
- Tourists, known as "leaf peepers," driving along Vermont's scenic roadways in autumn
- Dairy farms and apple orchards
- Rock quarries

Vermont is many things wrapped up in a small package. Turn the page to discover Vermont's unique people, places, and history.

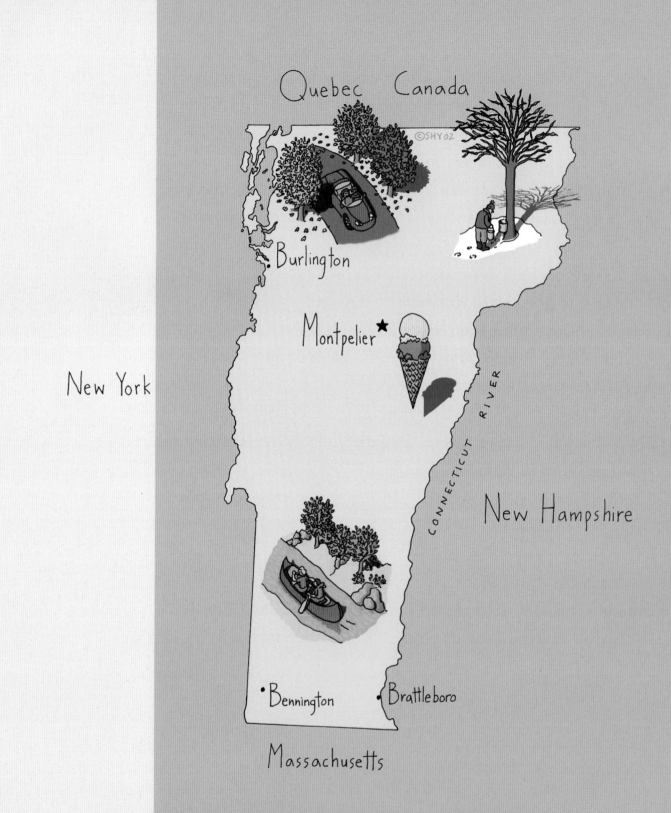

Quebec   Canada

©SHY02

• Burlington

New York

Montpelier ★

CONNECTICUT RIVER

New Hampshire

• Bennington   • Brattleboro

Massachusetts

CHAPTER TWO

THE LAND OF VERMONT

Vermont is in the northeastern part of the United States. New Hampshire borders Vermont to the east, Massachusetts is to the south, and New York lies to the west. Another country, Canada, borders Vermont to the north. Part of the border Vermont shares with New York lies in the middle of Lake Champlain, with half of the lake belonging to each state. The Connecticut River forms Vermont's border with New Hampshire. Vermont is the only New England state without an ocean border.

If you look at Vermont on a map, you will see it is roughly triangular in shape. The state is 157 miles (253 kilometers) long. At the Canadian border it is 90 miles (145 km) wide. The southern "point" of the triangle is the Massachusetts border, which is only 42 miles (68 km) wide.

Vermont's land has changed over the centuries due to glaciers, or huge sheets of ice, covering it and then slowly melting and receding. The

The Vermont landscape is made up of green fields, rolling hills, and tall mountains.

A maple sugar house is nestled in the hills of Vermont.

Green Mountains were probably much higher before the glaciers wore them down more than 10,000 years ago.

Today Vermont's landscape is incredibly varied. It has tall mountains and lush valleys, and more than 400 lakes and many rivers and streams. It even has islands. There are six distinct land regions in Vermont: the Champlain Valley, the Northeast Kingdom, the Vermont Piedmont, the Vermont Valley, the Taconic Range, and the Green Mountains.

THE CHAMPLAIN VALLEY

The Champlain Valley is in the northwestern part of Vermont, between Lake Champlain and the Green Mountains. The Champlain Valley has the flattest land in Vermont. In fact, this region is sometimes referred to as the Vermont Lowlands. The lowlands contain excellent soil and are home to many of Vermont's apple orchards and dairy farms. Corn, hay, oats, and wheat are also grown in this region.

Pastures dotted with dairy cows are a familiar sight in the Champlain Valley.

Boating on Lake Champlain is a favorite pastime for many people who live in Burlington.

FIND OUT MORE

The Chazyan Coral Reef is visible on Isle La Motte and spans 1,000 acres (405 hectares) under the island. It is said to be the oldest coral reef in the world, possibly 450 million years old. What is a coral reef made of? How is it formed?

Burlington, Vermont's largest city, is in the Champlain Valley. Many natural regions—undisturbed, protected acres of wetlands, forests, and geologic areas—exist in and around Burlington. Geologists from all over the world visit the Redstone Quarry Natural Area, which is located within the Burlington city limits. There scientists study ancient rocks, such as red quartzite, that were once on the bottom of a shallow ocean that covered this region centuries ago.

At the north end of the Champlain Valley, about 27 miles (43 km) from Canada, lies a land chain that includes the Alburg Peninsula (a peninsula is a finger of land surrounded by water on three sides), three large islands—Isle La Motte, North Hero, and Grand Isle—and many smaller ones. These are the Champlain Islands. The largest islands are populated, and their flat land boasts farms, apple orchards, and vineyards. The islands are rich in natural resources, too. Limestone and marble were once taken from island quarries (places where stone is dug or blasted out) and used in constructing everything from simple farmhouses to large buildings in Rockefeller Center, a New York City landmark.

NORTHEAST KINGDOM

The Northeast Kingdom covers a very small portion in the northeast corner of the state. Canada is directly to the north and New Hampshire lies to the east. The glaciers that covered the northeastern United States more than 12,000 years ago carved the land in this part of Vermont. This region has rounded, rolling hills and many forests. The mountains in the Northeast Kingdom are not as high as those in other parts of the state. Exceptions are Jay Peak and Burke Mountain, two popular ski areas in this region. The mountains in the Northeast Kingdom are made primarily of granite.

A skier takes in the view from a trail on Jay Peak.

WHO'S WHO IN VERMONT?

Perry Merrill (1894–1993) is known as the "patron saint of the ski industry." With his help, Vermont received workers and money as part of a government project known as the Civilian Conservation Corps (CCC). In the 1930s, the CCC was responsible for building ski trails in Vermont that were the foundation for much of today's ski industry.

About 117 square miles (303 square kilometers) of the Northeast Kingdom is public forest and park land. More than 1,000 additional square miles (2,590 sq km) are privately owned. Some areas have no roads because the terrain is so rugged, but much of this region can be explored on hiking and biking trails as well as by snowmobile.

In the past, large paper manufacturers owned timberlands in the Northeast Kingdom. Logging was once big business here. Today, many paper manufacturers have left Vermont, and the land they once logged is being conserved, or protected.

The many lakes, streams, and rivers make this part of Vermont a good place to hunt and fish. Deer and black bear are common, as well as salmon and lake trout.

VERMONT PIEDMONT

The area south of the Northeast Kingdom and east of the Green Mountains is called the Vermont Piedmont. This is the state's largest geographic region. *Piedmont* means "foot of the mountains" in French, so it is an appropriate name for this region, which lies at the foot of the Green Mountains.

The land in the Vermont Piedmont slopes down from the Green Mountains, forming rolling hills to the terraces or slopes along the Connecticut River. A lake covered this region after the glaciers melted and receded, forming these steps in the land.

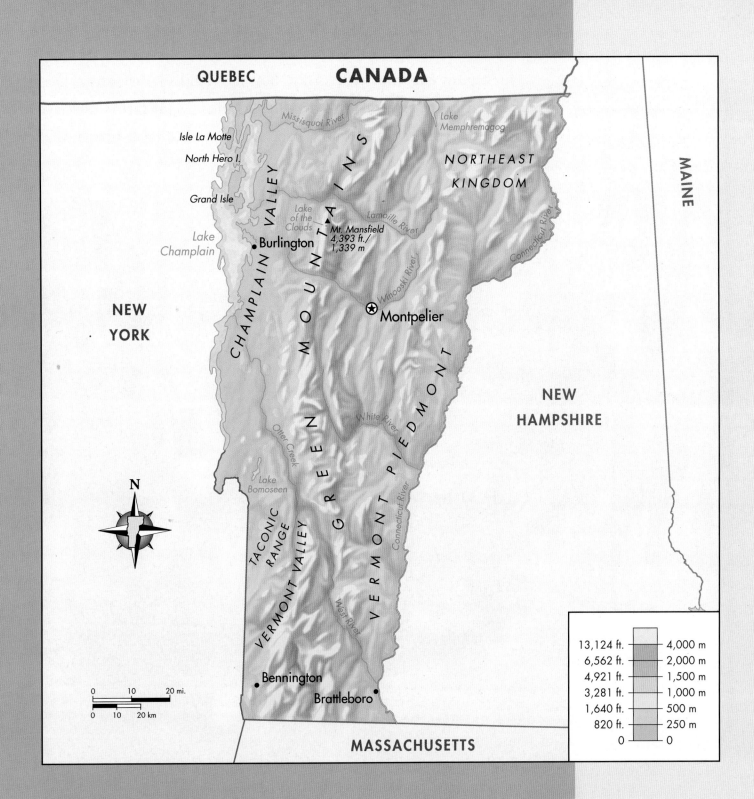

QUEBEC **CANADA**

Missisquoi River

Lake Memphremagog

Isle La Motte

North Hero I.

Grand Isle

CHAMPLAIN VALLEY

Lake Champlain

NORTHEAST KINGDOM

Lake of the Clouds

▲ Mt. Mansfield 4,393 ft./ 1,339 m

Lamoille River

Connecticut River

● Burlington

MAINE

Winooski River

GREEN MOUNTAINS

NEW YORK

☆ Montpelier

VERMONT PIEDMONT

NEW HAMPSHIRE

White River

Otter Creek

Lake Bomoseen

Connecticut River

N

TACONIC RANGE

VERMONT VALLEY

West River

● Bennington

Brattleboro ●

	13,124 ft.	4,000 m
	6,562 ft.	2,000 m
	4,921 ft.	1,500 m
	3,281 ft.	1,000 m
	1,640 ft.	500 m
	820 ft.	250 m
	0	0

0 10 20 mi.

0 10 20 km

MASSACHUSETTS

This region contains some of the best farmland in Vermont. There are dairy farms, fruit farms, and even llama farms. Many farms also have sugarhouses, where maple syrup is produced from the sugar maples that grow there.

With the help of two horses and a sledge, a Vermont family collects sap from sugar maples.

The Connecticut River meets the West River near the largest town in Vermont, Brattleboro. Brattleboro is close to the mountains in all directions. Farmers bring their goods to market in Brattleboro.

The lakes, rivers, and marshlands in this part of the state are home to many kinds of animals. Raccoons, otters, and beavers live there. Native peoples settled near the rivers to fish for salmon and shad long before the Europeans discovered Vermont.

Beavers live in the wetlands of Vermont.

THE VERMONT VALLEY

If you think of Vermont as a triangle, the Vermont Valley is at the southern point of the triangle. It is the area south of Brandon, a town in central Vermont, and north of the Massachusetts border. This region is only about 75 miles (121 km) long and is very narrow. In some places, it is less than a mile (1.6 km) wide. The Vermont Valley is made up of small river valleys, such as that of Battenkill River.

The Vermont Valley is famous for its marble quarries. The high-quality marble found there was used in the construction of the United Nations building in New York City and the Supreme Court building in Washington, D.C., as well as in many other buildings throughout the United States.

EXTRA! EXTRA!

The native people who settled in North America were the first Americans to make maple syrup, which they called *sinzibukwud*, or "sweet buds." They taught the first European settlers how to make maple syrup. Today, Vermont produces more maple syrup than any other state.

Marble is extracted from the ground in huge blocks.

THE TACONIC RANGE

The Taconic Range extends along the border between Vermont and New York, south of the Champlain Valley and into Massachusetts. The Taconic Mountains are part of the Appalachian Mountains, which are thought to be the oldest mountains in North America and extend from Canada to northern Alabama. The Taconics were formed more than 400 billion years ago. Because they are so old, the mountains have been worn down by centuries of erosion. Mount Equinox is the Taconics' tallest peak. It stands 3,816 feet (1,163 meters) above sea level.

The Taconics are made up of a variety of rocks such as limestone, marble, and slate. In Bennington, located in the southwest corner of this region, there are large deposits of clay. When the clay is dug up (mined), it is used to make dishes and other pottery products.

THE GREEN MOUNTAINS

The Green Mountain chain extends down the middle of Vermont, from Canada in the north to Massachusetts in the south. The Green Mountains are also part of the Appalachians. Granite, marble, and slate are quarried in these mountains.

The highest peaks in Vermont are part of the Green Mountains. Five of the peaks are more than 4,000 feet (1,219 m) high. The highest is Mount Mansfield, at 4,380 feet (1,336 m). Killington Peak

FIND OUT MORE

Draw a map showing where the Appalachian Mountains begin and end. What Canadian provinces and American states do they pass through?

EXTRA! EXTRA!

Near the town of Pownal is the Tri-state Monument. It marks the exact spot where New York, Vermont, and Massachusetts meet.

The summit of Mount Mansfield is the highest point in the state.

(4,226 feet/1,288 m); Mount Ellen (4,049 feet/1,235 m); and Camels Hump (4,065 feet/1,240 m) are other high peaks in the Green Mountains. Over the centuries, water and wind have cut through the mountains, forming spectacular gaps and notches, or gorges. Smuggler's Notch is the most well-known of these notches and is a destination for many visitors to Vermont.

Various types of trees such as pine, spruce, beech, and birch grow on the mountainsides. The sugar maple is best known for its sap, which is used to make maple syrup. It is the state tree of Vermont and is very colorful in the autumn.

The Green Mountains are known primarily as the heart of Vermont's tourist industry. More than 300,000 acres (121,406 ha) in the southern part of this region make up the Green Mountain National Forest. The forest is protected from development and offers year-round activities such as hiking, nature trails, and nature photography. The oldest hiking trail in the country passes the length of the Green Mountains. It is called the Long Trail and is 265 miles (426 km) long.

Many ski centers are located in the Green Mountains. Killington, the second highest mountain in Vermont, has the largest ski resort in the east. Other popular resorts include Stowe, Sugarbush, and Pico.

The spectacular colors of Green Mountain National Forest attract many visitors during the fall season.

RIVERS AND LAKES

In Vermont, rivers and lakes are almost as abundant as mountains. There are more than 400 lakes and ponds in the state. They are the settings for beautiful scenery, boating, fishing, canoeing, kayaking, and, in the winter, snowmobiling.

Lake Champlain is situated between the scenic beauty of New York's Adirondack Mountains and the Green Mountains of Vermont.

FIND OUT MORE

There are five Great Lakes in the United States. Some Vermonters feel that Lake Champlain should be designated the sixth. What are the five Great Lakes? What argument can be made for making Lake Champlain one of the Great Lakes?

Vermont's largest lake is Lake Champlain, the sixth largest freshwater lake in the United States. It is long and narrow—only 12 miles (19 km) across at its widest point and 120 miles (193 km) long.

In some spots Lake Champlain is 400 feet (122 m) deep. Some unusual and rare fish, such as longnose gar and bowfin, live in the lake. They are often called living fossils because they are descended from fish that are extinct everywhere else.

The second largest lake in Vermont, Lake Memphremagog, is in the Northeast Kingdom and forms part of Vermont's boundary with Canada. Only about a quarter of the lake is in Vermont.

The largest lake entirely within the state is Lake Bomoseen, near Rutland. Lake of the Clouds, located on Mount Mansfield, is the state's highest lake at 3,927 feet (1,198 m) above sea level.

Otter Creek, the longest river in Vermont, flows north into Lake Champlain. Most rivers in Vermont flow down the eastern slopes of the Green Mountains into the Connecticut River, or down the western side of the mountains into Lake Champlain. There are three rivers that flow directly through the Green Mountains and have cut deep gorges to accommodate their flow. These rivers are the Missisquoi River, the Lamoille River, and the Winooski River. The Winooski Valley is especially

A canoe trip on Otter Creek is a great way to take in the Vermont scenery.

scenic, and at 4,000 feet (1,219 m) deep, some people feel it rivals parts of Arizona's famous Grand Canyon for beauty.

CLIMATE

When you think of Vermont weather, you may picture lots of snow for skiing or other winter activities. What you may not realize is that Vermont has average summer temperatures of 69.5° Fahrenheit (20.8° Celsius).

Vermont has some extreme temperatures, with the coldest readings in the mountains and the Northeast Kingdom. In general, the valleys are warmer, with the warmest temperatures closest to Lake Champlain.

The average snowfall during a Vermont winter ranges from 60 to 100 inches (152 to 254 centimeters), although some mountain areas may receive up to 120 inches (305 cm). Snowfall is extremely important to the ski industry. If enough snow doesn't fall, most ski resorts must make their own.

CHAPTER THREE

VERMONT THROUGH HISTORY

The first people came to the area that is now Vermont about 10,500 years ago. They were Paleo (old or ancient) Indians who came from Asia by crossing an ancient land bridge into what is now Alaska. Paleo Indians were nomads who did not settle in one place but traveled where they found good hunting. They followed herds of woolly mammoth, elk, and other prey. They lived and hunted on the shores of lakes and rivers, then moved along with the animal herds.

Paleo Indians eventually stopped following the herds and settled down into permanent settlements. Their descendents in Vermont are the Abenaki. They were an Algonquian-speaking tribe.

The Abenaki lived in permanent settlements to the east and

Busy workers produce maple sugar at a maple sugar camp in early Vermont.

EXTRA! EXTRA!

Algonquian is a family of related languages with different dialects, or words and pronunciations. Algonquin is the name of a Native American tribe. However, not every tribe that spoke the Algonquian language was part of the Algonquin tribe.

west of the Green Mountains for thousands of years before the Europeans arrived. There is evidence that another group of Native Americans, the Mahicans ("Wolf People"), settled at the mouth of the Winooski River and around Missisquoi Bay. Evidence of Abenaki villages has been dug up along the Lake Champlain shoreline.

The Abenaki lived primarily in northern Vermont, New Hampshire, and Maine. Their largest village was near Swanton at the mouth of the

Early Native Americans in Vermont built canoes made of birchbark.

Missisquoi River, not far from Canada. They called themselves Abanal, meaning "men." They grew crops such as corn, beans, and squash, and they fished and hunted for food. Before the 1500s, the Abenaki tribe, which included the Pennacook and Micmac tribes, may have had a population of around 40,000. Today, Abenaki descendents live south of Swanton in St. Albans. The Abenaki population in Vermont and New Hampshire is estimated to be around 2,500.

EUROPEAN EXPLORERS

In 1609, Samuel de Champlain, a French fur trader and explorer, traveled from Quebec, Canada, to the lake that now bears his name, Lake Champlain. Champlain was sent to North America by King Henri IV of France. He is often given credit for "discovering" the lake, although native people lived there for thousands of years before he arrived. As a result of Champlain's trip, Vermont was made part of a territory called New France, which also included Quebec and Montreal. The territory was populated by natives and French settlers, mainly fur trappers.

WHAT'S IN A NAME?

Many place names in Vermont have interesting origins.

Name	Comes From or Means
Missisquoi	An Abenaki word meaning "pieces of flint"
Winooski	An Abenaki word meaning "wild onion"
Lake Memphremagog	An Abenaki word meaning "beautiful waters"
Mount Monadnock	An Abenaki word meaning "sticks up like an island"
Dog River	According to legend, this river near Montpelier got its name when a bear hunter caught his own dog in a trap by mistake
Milton	Named for English poet John Milton
Terrible Mountain	Refers to the fact that there is no trail across the mountaintop; it is impassable
Montpelier	A French word meaning "the most favored spot"

Samuel de Champlain was the first European to arrive in what is now Vermont.

At the time, France was very involved in the fur trade in Canada. Beaver fur was valuable in Europe, where it was made into hats. Champlain came to Vermont to build a settlement, so that the French could expand their fur trading with the Abenaki and another native tribe, the Iroquois. Both tribes traded with the French, who gave them household goods such as blankets and cooking pots in exchange for furs.

The Iroquois and the Abenaki did not get along, and they competed with each other for more trade with the French. Samuel de Champlain sided with the Abenaki because they were Algonquians, and peaceful relations with them would help prevent Algonquian attacks on French settlements in Quebec. Champlain gave the Abenaki new weapons—guns. He and his men helped them to fight the Iroquois, whose only weapons were bows and arrows. Thanks to their new weapons, the Abenaki won easily, driving the Iroquois back to the opposite side of Lake Champlain.

Champlain helped the Abenaki defeat the Iroquois in part to promote Abenaki fur trading with the French.

In 1666, the French built a fort on Isle La Motte, one of Vermont's islands in the northern end of Lake Champlain. They wanted to protect their trading routes from Iroquois attacks. The military post, called Fort St. Anne, was Vermont's first French settlement, although it did not flourish. The French eventually established more posts farther south, including a trading post at Chimney Point. Lake Champlain was used to transport fur and other goods to and from trading posts in Vermont and French settlements in Canada.

Residents of Fort Dummer prepare for an attack by Native Americans.

THE FRENCH AND INDIAN WAR

The British also settled in the area around Vermont, primarily in present-day Massachusetts, New Hampshire, and New York. They, too, were involved in the fur trade and wanted Lake Champlain for themselves. In 1724, the British built a fort west of the Connecticut River near what is now Brattleboro. They called it Fort Dummer. Its purpose was to protect British settlers in Massachusetts from raids by the Abenaki and the French. At this time, Vermont was mainly a passageway for French and Native American raiding parties who attacked British settlements to the south and east.

In 1754, the British and the French officially went to war over territorial rivalries. Both countries wanted to control the land in what is now the eastern United States. The French and Indian War (1754–1763) was widespread, including areas in New England, New York, Virginia, and the Ohio River Valley. Both the French and the British had Native American allies. In the northeast, the Abenaki sided with the French, and the Iroquois sided with the British. The war ended in 1763 with the signing of the Treaty of Paris, which gave Britain all French claims east of the Mississippi, including Vermont. As a result, Britain gained control of Lake Champlain and its trading routes.

THE NEW HAMPSHIRE LAND GRANTS

By 1764, the British colonies of New York and New Hampshire both claimed ownership of Vermont. Many years earlier, in 1749, King George II of Britain gave Benning Wentworth, the governor of New Hampshire, permission to issue "grants," or parcels of land, to British settlers from New Hampshire. The king told Wentworth to let the people settle in the land west of New Hampshire, but he never said exactly how far west. The land Wentworth made available to settlers was called the New Hampshire Land Grants.

At the same time, the governor of New York, George Clinton, was making grants to the east of his colony's borders—the same land that Wentworth had granted to New Hampshire settlers. This caused some problems, as both

Benning Wentworth's land grants were the start of what would later become Vermont.

WHO'S WHO IN VERMONT?

Ethan Allen (1738–1789) was born in Connecticut and moved to what is now Vermont in 1769. In 1775, he organized the Green Mountain Boys and proceeded to drive settlers from New York out of Vermont. Allen played an important role during the American Revolution, when he was instrumental in the capture of Fort Ticonderoga from the British in 1775.

New Yorkers and New Hampshirites laid claim to the same lands. In 1770, the king of Britain ruled that the land officially belonged to New York.

However, colonists from New Hampshire felt they had a right to the land, and they were angry with the king's decision. They decided to throw out the "Yorkers." In 1775, they formed a small militia (a volunteer army) of around 200 men called the Green Mountain Boys. Their leader was a man named Ethan Allen.

The Green Mountain Boys ran New York settlers off their land and burned their homes and businesses. They took back the land by force, and the governor of New York called them outlaws.

THE REVOLUTIONARY WAR

At the same time that the Green Mountain Boys were rebelling against the king's decision, the people of the thirteen colonies were rebelling against the British government, represented by the king himself. Tired of being overtaxed and ruled by the tyrannical British, the colonists eventually fought for freedom from Britain. This war was called the American Revolution (1775–1783).

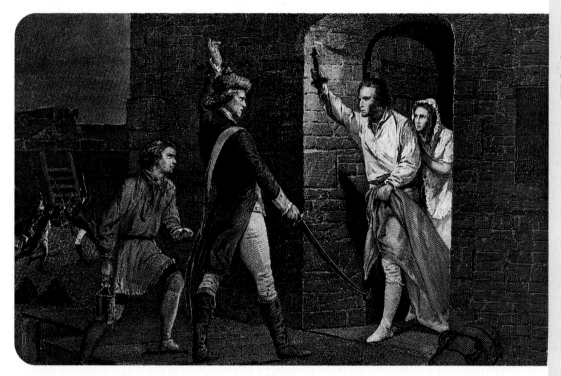

The Green Mountain Boys participated in one of the first skirmishes (small battles) of the war. In May 1775, they seized Fort Ticonderoga from the British. The fort, located at the southern tip of Lake Champlain in New York, was taken without a single bullet being fired. Ethan Allen and his men caught the British off guard. The Green Mountain Boys then moved north and took over the British post at Crown Point. They fought in the Battle of Hubbardton, where they helped stop the British from overtaking American soldiers leaving Fort Ticonderoga. Ethan Allen and his band were also present at the Battle of Bennington, which—although it is named for Bennington, Vermont—was actually fought in New York. British troops led by General John Burgoyne were

on their way to Bennington but were stopped in New York by John Stark and his men.

By the time the American Revolution ended in 1783, the British had been defeated. The newly independent United States was formed, but Vermont was not one of the original thirteen states. The United States Congress would not recognize Vermont as a state because of its disagreement with New York over land rights.

THE REPUBLIC OF VERMONT

Although many settlers in the region were actively battling the British for their independence, others still hoped to settle the question of the New Hampshire Land Grants. Since the New York settlers had been successfully driven off, many Vermonters felt it was time to separate from both New York and New Hampshire. On January 14, 1777, Vermont declared itself an independent republic. It was originally called New Connecticut, but the name was changed five months later to Vermont. The republic of Vermont had its own money and postal service. It handled its own affairs with foreign governments. Its constitution, or set of laws, was the first to prohibit slavery (the owning of one person by another person) and to guarantee all men the right to vote. Vermonters elected Thomas Chittenden president of the republic in 1778.

The Continental Congress, the governing body of the newly formed United States, largely ignored Vermont until a disagreement arose about where its borders were. New York, New Hampshire, and Connecticut all thought they had rights to land in Vermont. The situation became so heated that some members of the Continental Congress favored invading Vermont. They were talked out of it by George Washington, who would soon become the first president of the United States. The dispute was finally settled in 1790, when Vermont paid $30,000 for the land it had taken by force. In 1791, Vermont became the fourteenth state. Montpelier was chosen as the capital in 1805. The statehouse was constructed in 1808, and it remains the center of Vermont's government today.

After statehood, small communities such as this one developed all over Vermont.

THE STATE OF VERMONT

Vermont's population grew rapidly in the years following its admission to the United States. By 1810, the population was more

Early Vermont farms grew apple trees, whose apples were then processed and turned into cider.

than 200,000. French Canadians moved down from Quebec and settled near Lake Champlain. Scottish immigrants came across the Atlantic Ocean to work in the rock quarries, and the Irish came to Vermont to work on canals. Many newcomers came from other New England states to start farms in Vermont.

Vermont's natural resources were important to its newly developing industries. Paper mills and sawmills were constructed next to swiftly moving streams to harness their energy. Logs were floated down the Connecticut River to paper mills, and up Lake Champlain to Canada. The lake was an important route for getting goods and people where they wanted to go. By 1808, steamboats were a familiar sight on Lake Champlain and the Connecticut River.

While industries were developing in Vermont, the state also gained an agricultural identity. Many early Vermonters were sheep farmers. Sheep not only provided wool, but also led to supporting industries such as tanneries (places to make sheepskin into leather) and mills to process wool into yarn.

THE WAR OF 1812

During the early 1800s, Britain and France were at war. The United States tried to remain neutral, but when both Britain and France raided and seized American ships, it was time to take action. In 1807, President Thomas Jefferson signed a law called the Embargo Act that stopped trade with all foreign countries. In 1809, the law was changed to prevent trade with Britain and France only. Vermonters did not like these laws, because they often traded with Canada, which was a British colony.

The United States declared war against Britain in 1812. The War of 1812 (1812–1815), was very unpopular in Vermont. Some residents of northern Vermont, nearest Canada, abandoned their land in fear of a British invasion from the north. Others, however, profited from the war. Smugglers secretly moved beef and other food products from Vermont to Canada. Sheep farmers profited as the demand for wool rose, because wool was used to make blankets and uniforms for the American army. In 1813, a fleet of ships was built in Vergennes, Vermont, and used in the Battle of Plattsburgh in New York. This battle was won by the Americans and gave control of Lake Champlain to the United States. When the war ended in 1815, trade between Britain and the United States resumed.

THE CIVIL WAR

Becoming a state did not change the way the people of Vermont felt about slavery. They didn't like the idea of people paying money for and

owning other people, who were called slaves. Starting in the 1600s, Africans were kidnapped from their native lands and brought to the United States on ships. Many of them were forced to work on large farms called plantations. By the 1800s, slavery was commonplace in the South. Most Northerners, however, were against this practice. According to Vermont's constitution, slavery was illegal in the state.

In 1860, a native Vermonter, Stephen Douglas, ran for president against Abraham Lincoln and two other candidates. Lincoln vowed to stop the spread of slavery to new territories. Vermonters voted in overwhelming numbers for Lincoln.

Stephen Douglas and Abraham Lincoln participated in public debates while running for president.

Because slavery was illegal in the North, many enslaved Africans took the chance of escaping to northern states and Canada on the Underground Railroad. This wasn't a real train, but a series of places where every-day people sheltered escaping Africans before sending them on safely to the next stop. Vermont was active in this effort. Some escaped Africans settled in Vermont, while others continued on to Canada.

The disagreement between North and South contributed to the outbreak of the Civil War (1861–1865). The Union (the North) fought against the Confederacy (the South). Vermont was the first northern state to provide troops for the Civil War. More than 35,000 men from Vermont served in the war.

WHO'S WHO IN VERMONT?

Stephen Douglas (1813–1861) was born in Brandon, Vermont, but moved to Illinois, where he became a United States representative (1843–1847) and a United States senator (1847–1861). In 1860, he ran for president against Abraham Lincoln and was defeated. Douglas believed that each state should be able to make their own decisions on issues such as slavery.

Members of a Vermont Civil War regiment pose for a picture.

There were no battles on Vermont soil, but the northernmost incident of the war took place there. In 1864, a band of Confederate soldiers robbed three banks in St. Albans. They ran across the border to Canada, where most of them were captured by Canadian authorities.

When the Civil War ended, the North was victorious. More than 600,000 men had died; 5,000 came from tiny Vermont.

THE INDUSTRIAL REVOLUTION

After the Civil War, most of the northern states grew in population, and industry flourished. This time of prosperity was called the Industrial Revolution because in many areas the emphasis shifted from agriculture to industry. Big cities such as New York, Boston, and Chicago grew in leaps and bounds. Vermont saw its share of changes, too. Farming declined as Vermonters realized that overgrazing by sheep and overplanting of crops year after year had depleted what was once rich topsoil. Some farmers moved west to start over, and others moved to Massachusetts and New York to take jobs in newly built factories.

There was some growth in Vermont in the 1870s and 1880s as the wood-processing

During the 1800s, almost every Vermont village had at least one cheese manufacturer.

38

and cheesemaking industries flourished. Burlington became a hub for timber imported from Canada, and lumber exported to the rest of the United States. Thaddeus Fairbanks put St. Johnsbury on the map after inventing the platform scale, a device used to measure weight. The invention tripled the state's population when a factory for making scales was built there.

Vermont's first railroad was completed in 1848. It was part of a larger line that ran from Boston to the Great Lakes. The railroad industry continued to grow. In the 1870s, Rutland became a major railroading center. However, even with these advances, Vermont never saw the industrialization that brought prosperity to other areas of the Northeast.

THE EARLY 1900S

In 1914, World War I (1914–1918) started in Europe. The United States entered the war in April, 1917. Vermont's state legislature set aside one million dollars for the war effort, and at least 16,000 Vermonters served in World War I. The best known is Admiral Henry T. Mayo of Burlington, who served as commander in chief of the Atlantic fleet.

When the war was over, Vermont found itself in battle yet again—with Mother Nature. In 1927, record-breaking rainfalls began in October and continued into early November. By November 4, many of the

During World War I, more than 8,000 men were stationed at Fort Ethan Allen in Colchester, Vermont.

state's rivers had flooded the towns built along their banks. In the state capital, Montpelier, as well as in other towns and villages, floodwaters rose to second-story heights. Many houses were swept away, and 85 people died. The flood of 1927 is considered the worst natural disaster in Vermont's history.

The flood of 1927 destroyed homes, bridges, and railroad tracks in Vermont.

THE GREAT DEPRESSION

In 1929, the stock market "crashed." People all across the country, including Vermont, lost huge amounts of money on their business investments. As a result, they could not afford to buy goods, and many industries failed. Banks closed. Many people lost money, jobs, or

EXTRA! EXTRA!

Native Vermonter Calvin Coolidge (right) became president of the United States in 1923, after President Warren G. Harding died in office. Vice president Coolidge took the oath of office in his boyhood home in Plymouth, Vermont, on August 2, 1923. Coolidge was not the first Vermonter to succeed to the presidency (become president without being voted in).
In July 1881, after President James Garfield was assassinated (killed), vice president and Vermont native Chester A. Arthur served out Garfield's term.

both. They lost homes and businesses. Many Vermonters were forced to take aid from the government, as did others throughout the country. This period is known as the Great Depression (1929–1939).

To help put people back to work, the United States government put money into many projects in Vermont and elsewhere. The Civilian Conservation Corps (CCC) was created for this purpose. In Vermont, more than 40,000 men were put to work building roads, dams, parks, and ski slopes. The ski trails that they put in place laid the groundwork for the booming ski industry that exists in Vermont today.

Stowe became a successful ski resort after 1933, when the CCC cut a 4-mile (6.4-km) trail down the mountain.

WORLD WAR II

World War II (1939–1945) began on September 1, 1939, when Germany invaded Poland. The United States did not enter the war until December, 1941, when Japan attacked a United States military base at Pearl Harbor in Hawaii.

The Great Depression ended when the United States entered World War II. Along with the war came an increase in industry to meet the needs of the military. Many Vermonters left the state to find jobs in

Massachusetts and Connecticut factories. Others stayed put and worked in the Shelburne Shipyards, where they built torpedo patrol boats. Others found employment in Springfield making machine tools. Many of these employees were women, going to work for the first time to take the place of men who were now busy defending their country. Of the 50,000 Vermont citizens who served in the military in World War II, more than 12,000 died.

Many women joined the workforce for the first time during World War II.

VERMONT BOOMS

After World War II, the United States prospered. Jobs were plentiful. Many babies were born as men who returned from war married, carried on careers, and began raising families. All of this was good for the economy.

Things were also good in Vermont. The population increased and continued to grow in the fifty years after the war. New industries such as computer manufacturing and electronics attracted people to the state.

Large-scale expansion of recreational facilities such as ski resorts accounted for much of Vermont's

FAMOUS FIRSTS

- Vermont's Concord Academy was the first school devoted to training future teachers. It was opened in 1823 by Reverend Samuel Hall.
- The first postage stamp used in the United States was made in Brattleboro in 1846.
- Consuelo Northrop Bailey from Fairfield was the first woman in the nation to be elected lieutenant governor of Vermont in 1954.
- Dr. H. Nelson Jackson of Burlington was the first person to cross the entire United States by automobile in 1902.
- The first school to provide higher education for women was started by Emma Willard in Middlebury in 1814.
- The first ski chairlift in New England was used on Mt. Mansfield in 1940.

growth. The state's slogan, "The Playground of the Continent," was being taken seriously. Ski trails popped up like mushrooms. Some farmers sold their land so people could build condominiums and housing developments. People continued to explore and settle in Vermont.

In the 1950s, construction of an interstate highway system was begun. The primary routes in Vermont are Interstate 89, which runs from the Canadian border in northwestern Vermont to White River Junction on the New Hampshire border; and Interstate 91, from the Massachusetts border to the Canadian border in northeastern Vermont. Highways such as these made Vermont easily accessible.

The "back to the land" movement in the 1960s and 1970s brought people to Vermont seeking a simple life. This movement grew out of a feeling that life in the United States had gotten too complex and dependent on money and possessions. The young people arriving in Vermont were enchanted by its beauty and rural atmosphere. They hoped to build their own homes, grow their own food, and live simple, productive lives.

MODERN VERMONT

The population growth, construction, and increased traffic brought concerns. Vermont's lakes and streams were becoming polluted, and its green space was disappearing. In 1970, the state's general assembly passed the Environmental Control Law. This law, commonly known as Act 250, forces land developers to prove that their project will not harm

Many Vermont towns use town meetings as a form of government. Citizens gather in a meeting hall to discuss issues of concern.

the environment in any way. Vermont was the first state to pass such a law. In 1988, the state also passed the Growth Management Act. Its purpose is to control growth and development to protect green space and natural resources.

The fast pace of development also worried Vermonters who wanted to protect their state's "small town" atmosphere. A basic part of what makes Vermont unique is the idea of small local governments with town meetings where everyone has a voice. This way of life has been threatened in recent years by large housing developments and chain stores opening up in the state. Some Vermonters have been disturbed by this change to their society and vow to "Take Back Vermont," turning back the clock to simpler times.

The 1970s, 1980s, and 1990s saw the electronic and computer industries grow and prosper in Vermont. Tourism continues to grow and expand as the state remains a destination for visitors the world over. Since Vermont began advertising its spectacular fall foliage in the late 1940s, the highways have been busy every October with "leaf peepers."

Vermonters have always been known for valuing their privacy and their independence. Through every major war, the Great Depression, and crushing winters, their "Yankee" spirit remains.

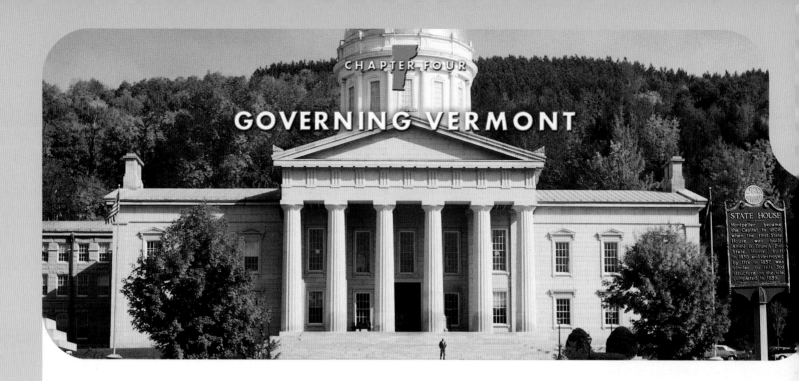

CHAPTER FOUR

GOVERNING VERMONT

STATE HOUSE
Montpelier became the Capital in 1808, when the first State House was built. Ammi B. Young's 2nd State House, built in 1838 and destroyed by fire in 1857, was similar to this 3rd structure on the site, completed in 1859.

From the time Vermont became a republic in 1777, it has taken its independence seriously. Even today, Vermont's government reflects the independent spirit it displayed in its early days. Its constitution, a document that lays down the basic laws and principles of the state, is patterned after the United States Constitution. Vermont's original constitution was adopted in 1777 and revised in 1786 and 1793. It was the first in the country to outlaw slavery. It was also the first to guarantee any male resident over the age of 21 the right to vote. The constitution may be amended, or changed, every four years.

Vermont has three branches of state government: the executive branch, the legislative branch, and the judicial branch. Each branch has its own specific duties. These branches work together to make sure that the state runs smoothly.

Vermont's state house is one of the oldest capitol buildings still in use.

EXECUTIVE BRANCH

The executive branch enforces and carries out the laws of the state. The governor is head of the executive branch. He or she works with the other branches of government, and deals with things like reducing crime, improving education, and balancing the state's budget. Vermonters elect their governor for a two-year term, but many governors serve more than one term in office. Other members of the executive branch are the lieutenant governor, the attorney general, the secretary of state, and the state treasurer. They are also elected for two years.

The Vermont house of representatives meets inside the capitol building.

LEGISLATIVE BRANCH

The legislative branch creates laws for the people of Vermont. They pass laws on a variety of subjects, such as laws to protect the environment or to improve the state's public schools.

The legislative branch is called the General Assembly. It is made up of two parts: the senate and the house of representatives. There are 30 senators and 150 representatives elected by the citizens of Vermont. The senate and the

VERMONT STATE GOVERNMENT

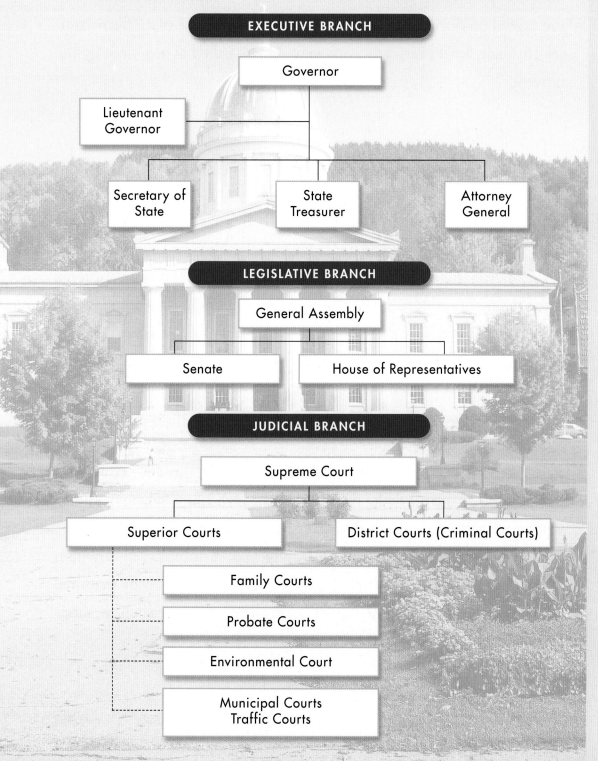

EXECUTIVE BRANCH

Governor

Lieutenant Governor

Secretary of State

State Treasurer

Attorney General

LEGISLATIVE BRANCH

General Assembly

Senate

House of Representatives

JUDICIAL BRANCH

Supreme Court

Superior Courts

District Courts (Criminal Courts)

Family Courts

Probate Courts

Environmental Court

Municipal Courts
Traffic Courts

house of representatives meet at the Vermont statehouse in Montpelier, the capital of Vermont. The meetings, or sessions, take place from January through April every year, but may also be called at any time by the governor.

JUDICIAL BRANCH

The judicial branch is responsible for determining the meaning of laws. The courts make up the judicial branch. If there is a disagreement over the laws, the courts have the final say.

Vermont's highest, or most important, court is the state supreme court. Its main job is to make sure the state court system is doing its job correctly. It makes sure that decisions made in lower courts are fair. The supreme court is made up of a chief justice (judge) and four associate justices. They are elected by the legislature for six-year terms.

There are fourteen counties in Vermont. Each one has a superior court. These courts hear civil cases, which have to do with people's rights. If someone feels he was treated unfairly by another person or a business, he or she may take their case to the civil court, where the judge will decide who is right. There are twelve superior court judges.

There are seventeen district court judges in Vermont, each of whom is appointed by the governor. District courts handle mostly criminal cases, those in which someone has committed a crime such as shoplifting or robbery.

VERMONT GOVERNORS

Name	Term	Name	Term
Thomas Chittenden	1778–1789	John L. Barstow	1882–1884
Moses Robinson	1789–1790	Samuel E. Pingree	1884–1886
Thomas Chittenden	1790–1797	Ebenezer J. Ormsbee	1886–1888
Paul Bingham	1797 (acting governor)	William P. Dillingham	1888–1890
		Carroll S. Page	1890–1892
Isaac Tichenor	1797–1807	Levi K. Fuller	1892–1894
Israel Smith	1807–1808	Urban A. Woodbury	1894–1896
Isaac Tichenor	1808–1809	Josiah Grout	1896–1898
Jonas Galusha	1809–1813	Edward C. Smith	1898–1900
Martin Chittenden	1813–1815	William W. Stickney	1900–1902
Jonas Galusha	1815–1820	John McCullough	1902–1904
Richard Skinner	1820–1823	Charles J. Bell	1904–1906
Cornelius P. Van Ness	1823–1826	Fletcher D. Proctor	1906–1908
Ezra Butler	1826–1828	George H. Prouty	1908–1910
Samuel C. Crafts	1828–1831	John A. Mead	1910–1912
William A. Palmer	1831–1835	Allen M. Fletcher	1912–1915
Silas H. Jennison	1835–1841	Charles W. Gates	1915–1917
Charles Paine	1841–1843	Horace F. Graham	1917–1919
John Mattocks	1843–1844	Percival W. Clement	1919–1921
William Slade	1844–1846	James Hartness	1921–1923
Horace Eaton	1846–1848	Redfield Proctor	1923–1925
Carlos Coolidge	1848–1850	Franklin S. Billings	1925–1927
Charles K. Williams	1850–1852	John E. Weeks	1927–1931
Erastus Fairbanks	1852–1853	Stanley C. Wilson	1931–1935
John S. Robinson	1853–1854	Charles M. Smith	1935–1937
Stephen Royce	1854–1856	George D. Aiken	1937–1941
Ryland Fletcher	1856–1858	William H. Wills	1941–1945
Hiland Hall	1858–1860	Mortimer R. Proctor	1945–1947
Erastus Fairbanks	1860–1861	Ernest W. Gibson	1947–1950
Frederick Holbrook	1861–1863	Harold J. Arthur	1950–1951
John Gregory Smith	1863–1865	Lee E. Emerson	1951–1955
Paul Dillingham	1865–1867	Joseph B. Johnson	1955–1959
John B. Page	1867–1869	Robert T. Stafford	1959–1961
Peter T. Washburn	1869–1870	F. Ray Keyser Jr.	1961–1963
George Hendee	1870 (acting governor)	Phillip H. Hoff	1963–1969
		Deane C. Davis	1969–1973
John W. Stewart	1870–1872	Thomas Salmon	1973–1977
Julius Converse	1872–1874	Richard Snelling	1977–1985
Asahel Peck	1874–1876	Madeline Kunin	1985–1991
Horace Fairbanks	1876–1878	Richard Snelling	1991
Redfield Proctor	1878–1880	Howard Dean	1991–2003
Roswell Farnham	1880–1882	Jim Douglas	2003–

Each county also has a family court and a probate court. Family court deals with problems that occur within families, such as divorce and child abuse. Probate court handles adoptions and helps to settle estates when someone dies.

The Traffic and Municipal Ordinance Bureau of Vermont deals with traffic violations and fish and game laws, such as hunting or fishing out of season or without a license. Vermont also has an environmental court with one judge. This court hears cases regarding zoning, planning, and natural resources.

Montpelier is known for its small size, historic neighborhoods, and its location in the heart of ski country.

TAKE A TOUR OF MONTPELIER, THE CAPITAL

Montpelier is located almost in the middle of the state near the Winooski River. It was chosen as the state capital because of its central location. Montpelier is small when compared with other capital cities. In fact, it has the smallest population of any state capital—about 8,000 people live there.

Montpelier has had three statehouses. The first was built in 1805. It was replaced in 1836 by a grand

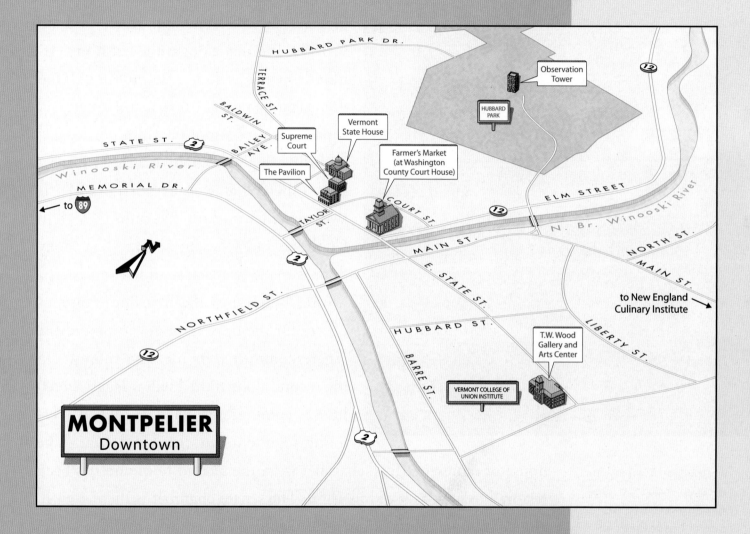

HUBBARD PARK DR.

Observation Tower

HUBBARD PARK

12

TERRACE ST.

BALDWIN ST.

STATE ST. 2

BAILEY AVE.

Supreme Court

Vermont State House

Farmer's Market (at Washington County Court House)

The Pavilion

Winooski River

MEMORIAL DR.

to 89

TAYLOR ST.

COURT ST.

12

ELM STREET

N. Br. Winooski River

2

MAIN ST.

E. STATE ST.

NORTH ST.

MAIN ST.

to New England Culinary Institute

NORTHFIELD ST.

HUBBARD ST.

LIBERTY ST.

12

BARRE ST.

T.W. Wood Gallery and Arts Center

VERMONT COLLEGE OF UNION INSTITUTE

MONTPELIER
Downtown

2

The reception room inside the capitol includes a large painting of the Civil War battle of Cedar Creek, in which Vermont troops participated.

structure that burned in 1857, leaving only a portico (a covered walk supported by columns). The portico was incorporated into the current statehouse, which was built in 1859. It is made of granite cut from Vermont's own quarries. The building's gold dome can be seen for miles, and a statue of Ethan Allen stands on the front portico.

Inside the main lobby is a bust of Abraham Lincoln, as well as portraits of the two presidents from Vermont, Calvin Coolidge and Chester Arthur. The lobby floor is made of black marble from Isle La Motte. The rest of the first floor contains offices for the lieutenant governor and the senate committee or meeting rooms. On the second floor is the Hall of Flags, which houses some of the flags carried by Vermont regiments in the Civil War. The house of representatives' chamber is on the second floor and has been restored to look as it did in 1859. The senate chamber is there as well, and contains all of its original furnishings. The governor's office is also on the second floor and features portraits of some of the governors who served the state during the 1800s.

Not far from the statehouse is the state supreme court building and the Pavilion Building. The Vermont Historical Society and Museum is in the Pavilion Building. The museum's exhibits show how the state has changed throughout history.

Montpelier is a college town. Vermont College is located on the site of a Civil War hospital. The work of many Vermont artists and craftspeople is displayed in the T. W. Wood Gallery & Art Center in College Hall. The New England Culinary Institute is also located in Montpelier. NECI, as it is called, turns out world-class chefs. It also owns and operates two

Although it is a small school, Vermont College attracts students from around the world.

restaurants and a bakery in Montpelier so that its students can benefit from hands-on experience.

The best view of Montpelier is from the 54-foot (16-m) observation tower in Hubbard Park. The park was a gift of John E. Hubbard, son of a wealthy Montpelier family. It is 185 acres (75 ha) large. The park has ski and hiking trails, soccer and baseball fields, and places to picnic—all within walking distance of downtown.

CHAPTER FIVE

THE PEOPLE AND PLACES OF VERMONT

Vermont is a small state that thinks big. With only 608,827 residents—the second lowest population of the fifty states—Vermont has a lot to offer. Its residents work in a variety of jobs and live in a region that offers mountains and lakes, skiing and hiking, and farms and high technology—all in one telephone area code.

The "Morris Ale" dancers prepare to perform morris dancing, a traditional English dance, in a small town in Vermont.

MEET THE PEOPLE

Vermont was settled mainly by people of French Canadian and British descent. In the 1800s, European immigrants came to Vermont to work in the granite and marble industries and on the railroads. Today, most Vermonters—almost 97 of every 100 people—are of European descent. Asians account for fewer than 1 in every 100 people, as do African Americans, Native Americans, and Hispanics.

Vermont has become slightly more diverse (having people of different ethnicities) over the past ten years. According to the 2000 census, 5,217 people in Vermont are of Asian descent, and approximately 3,000 are African-American. More than 5,500 Latinos and 2,420 Native Americans, most of them Abenaki, were counted. However, Vermont still has one of the smallest minority populations in the United States.

More than two-thirds of the population live in rural areas. The urban areas of Vermont are small compared with those of other states. Burlington is the largest city, with a population of almost 39,000. It is also one of the fastest-growing areas in Vermont, thanks to the booming tourist and electronics-manufacturing industries. Rutland (17,292) and South Burlington (15,814) are other large cities.

Residents of Rutland browse at an outdoor market downtown.

WORKING IN VERMONT

People in Vermont are employed in all kinds of jobs, but most of these jobs fall into three main categories: manufacturing, tourism, and agriculture. The manufacturing industry has grown steadily since the 1970s, and produces products such as headstones made from top-quality Vermont granite, machine tools such as drills and grinders, paper and paper products, food products such as milk, cheese, and maple syrup, and wood products such as furniture and hockey sticks. High-technology industries centered around Burlington have been successful in the last ten years, producing electronic circuitry, computer equipment, and software. IBM, General Electric, and Verizon are three international companies located in this area.

The tourist industry has grown and provided many jobs for Vermonters since the early 1900s. Ski resorts have cropped up in record numbers during the past 20 years, and fall foliage has become big business. Sugar shacks, where visitors can learn how maple sugar and syrup are made, are a common sight on the Vermont countryside. Vermonters who work in the tourist industry have many types of jobs. They may be tour guides, ski instructors, innkeepers, waiters and waitresses, storekeepers, cooks, and many other things. If you can imagine all the people you come in contact with on a vacation, you have an idea how big the tourist industry is in Vermont. For such a small state, there is a lot to see and do.

Tourism-related jobs are part of a larger industry called the service industry. Businesses in the service industry don't create a product; they

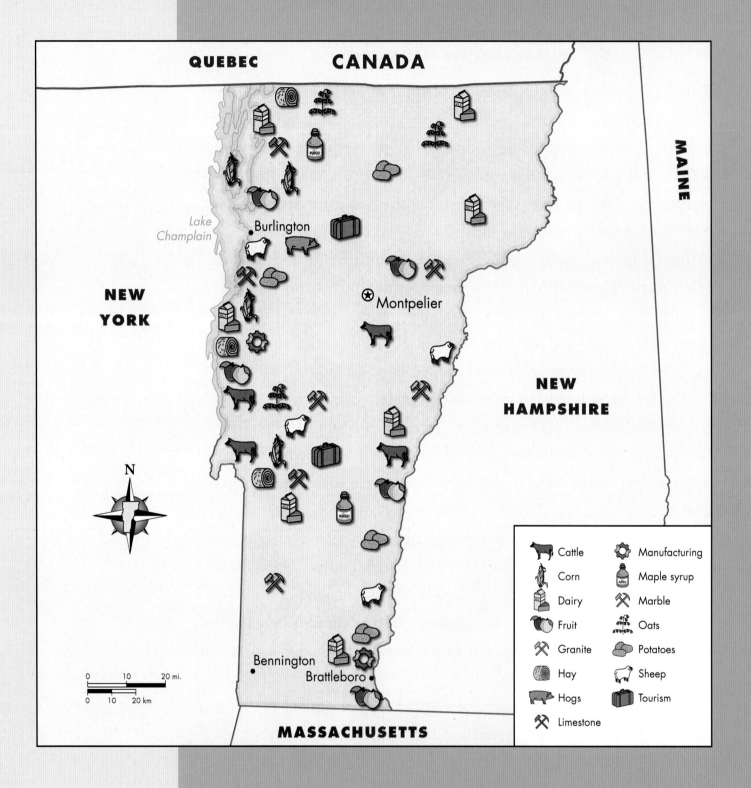

QUEBEC CANADA

MAINE

Lake
Champlain

• Burlington

NEW
YORK

⊛ Montpelier

NEW

HAMPSHIRE

N

• Bennington
Brattleboro •

0   10   20 mi.
0   10   20 km

MASSACHUSETTS

Cattle   Manufacturing
Corn   Maple syrup
Dairy   Marble
Fruit   Oats
Granite   Potatoes
Hay   Sheep
Hogs   Tourism
Limestone

provide a service. Vermonters in the service industry might work in retail (stores), insurance or real estate agencies, or transportation and utility companies such as telephone and electric companies. The service industry is largest in Vermont's big cities, such as Burlington and Rutland, as well as in Montpelier and other tourist areas.

A modern spin on the "back to the land" movement are the many home-based businesses that can be found in Vermont. Some people do business from home using computers and fax machines, while others are crafters, making saleable goods in their homes.

Many people work on farms in Vermont. In 1999, there were more than 6,000 farms in the state. More than 1 million acres (404,686 ha) are used for agriculture. Milk is one of Vermont's most important products.

EXTRA! EXTRA!

Many farmers in Vermont welcome visitors. You can sleep in a centuries-old farmhouse and wake up to a hearty farm breakfast. You can also help with the farm chores, pick strawberries and apples, or just take in the beautiful Vermont scenery.

A Vermont dairy farmer shows off a calf.

Two things that Vermont has a lot of are snow and maple syrup. Combine them and you have a tasty treat. Remember to ask an adult for help!

SUGAR ON SNOW

maple syrup
clean, fluffy, freshly fallen snow (a few handfuls)
dill pickle (optional)

1. Heat a small amount of maple syrup just to boiling.
2. Fill a bowl or a paper cup with clean, freshly fallen snow.
3. Pour hot maple syrup over the snow in the cup.
4. Try this if you dare: Take a bite of the sugar on snow and then a bite of a dill pickle. It's a Vermont tradition!

Other dairy products, such as ice cream and cheese, are also produced there. Vermont's climate makes it perfect for growing hay, apples, corn, and Christmas trees. It is the number-one producer of maple syrup and sugar in the United States.

Many of Vermont's farmers are diversifying—that is, exploring new products and ways to make money from their land. Some ways in which they do this are by growing organic vegetables, producing special kinds of cheese and yogurt, and turning parts of their homes into inns for vacationing families. Some farmers sell their land to land trusts, which, in turn, allow them to continue to farm it.

TAKE A TOUR OF VERMONT

Northern Vermont

A good place to start touring Vermont is the northwestern corner on the Champlain Islands. On Isle La Motte you can view the remains of Fort St. Anne, the oldest settlement in Vermont. The Royal Lipizzan Stallions, also known as the "flying white stallions," have their summer home on North Hero Island. These graceful and highly trained horses are known as the ballet dancers of the horse world.

Next, head south to Burlington, where you can visit Ethan Allen's 1787 farm. It has an education center, a multimedia show, and an interactive archeological exhibit. Burlington is full of things to see and do. Church Street Marketplace in downtown Burlington offers 130 shops, restaurants, and vendors. If you like chocolate, you'll love

With its historic atmosphere and charming shops, Burlington's Church Street Marketplace is one of the top tourist attractions in Vermont.

a tour of Lake Champlain Chocolates, where you can watch chocolate makers prepare the candy in small batches. Be sure to try a free sample!

Burlington is also home to the University of Vermont, the fifth-oldest university in New England. About 9,400 students are enrolled at the university. There is also a lot to see and do on campus, including museums, gardens, and art exhibits.

South of Burlington, in Shelburne, you can explore a 1,400-acre (567-ha) working farm and museum. You'll find everything there from a carousel to a lighthouse, and you can milk a cow if you want to. The Shelburne Museum includes 37 historic structures, including the steamboat *Ticonderoga* and a covered bridge. The Vermont Teddy Bear Factory is also in Shelburne. The factory ships handmade teddy bears to places all around the world. You can take a tour and watch the bears being made.

East of Shelburne, in Waterbury, you'll find Ben and Jerry's Ice Cream Factory. The tour will give you a behind-the-scenes look at how all those scrumptious flavors are made. You'll be able to taste-test some, too!

WHO'S WHO IN VERMONT?

Ben Cohen and Jerry Greenfield (1951–) founded Ben & Jerry's, Vermont's Finest Ice Cream and Frozen Yogurt, in 1978 in Burlington, Vermont. Their company became famous for its creative new flavors, all of which were made from Vermont milk and cream.

A tour of Ben and Jerry's Ice Cream Factory lets you see the ice cream production line in action.

A hop, skip, and a jump southeast of Waterbury is the state capital of Vermont, Montpelier. You can take a free tour of the statehouse every weekday. The Vermont Historical Society is also in Montpelier. During your visit, you'll find answers to questions such as: why are some bridges in New England covered, and what did the last panther in Vermont look like?

Northwest of Montpelier is Stowe. To many people, Stowe means skiing. Because it is near Mount Mansfield, the highest mountain in the state, Stowe is a natural ski destination. However, there are other attractions in Stowe, as well. The Trapp Family Lodge, where the famous von Trapp family settled after they left Austria during World War II, is in

Skiers wait for the lift at Mount Mansfield, near Stowe.

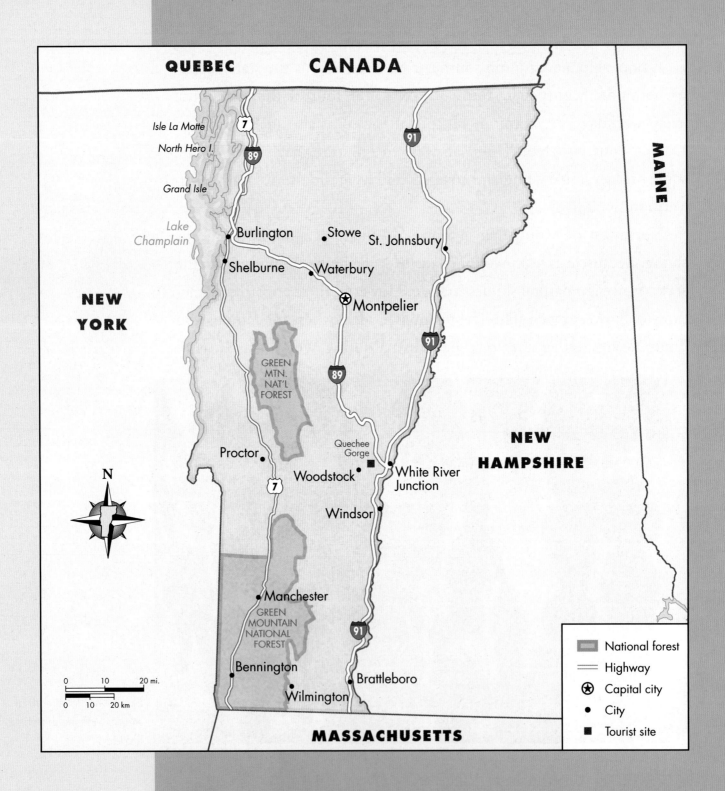

QUEBEC **CANADA**

Isle La Motte

North Hero I.

Grand Isle

Lake Champlain

7 **89** **91**

Burlington • Stowe • St. Johnsbury •

Shelburne • Waterbury •

NEW YORK

⊛ Montpelier

GREEN MTN. NAT'L FOREST

MAINE

89

91

Quechee Gorge

NEW HAMPSHIRE

Proctor •

Woodstock • ■ • White River Junction

7

Windsor •

N

Manchester •

GREEN MOUNTAIN NATIONAL FOREST

91

Bennington •

Brattleboro •

Wilmington •

0   10   20 mi.

0   10   20 km

MASSACHUSETTS

	National forest
	Highway
⊛	Capital city
•	City
■	Tourist site

Stowe. Summer concerts take place outside the lodge, and skiers roam the grounds in winter. You could also hike, drive, or take a gondola ride to the summit of Mount Mansfield.

The world's oldest and largest maple candy factory, The Original Maple Grove Maple Museum and Factory, is located in St. Johnsbury. Visitors can tour the factory and watch maple products being made and packed for shipping around the world.

Central Vermont

In Norwich you can explore space, nature, and technology at the Montshire Museum of Science. It features hands-on exhibits, aquariums, and outdoor hiking trails. Also in town is Norwich University. Founded in 1819, it is the oldest private military college in the United States. Many University students are enrolled in the Corps of Cadets, a program that provides training for military service. Others earn degrees in business, mathematics, engineering, and other subjects.

Quechee Gorge, south of Norwich, is sometimes called the Grand Canyon of the

Quechee Gorge was formed by the Ottauquechee River, which carved a gap into the hillside.

East. The area around the gorge was settled in the 1760s, when homesteaders built mills along the Ottauquechee River and used its energy to produce cider and lumber. Today, the village of Quechee thrives as a major tourist attraction.

West of Quechee Gorge, in Woodstock, you can take a step back in time at the Billings Farm and Museum. Reconstructed homes and a general store, a school, and a workshop give you an idea of what life was like in early Vermont.

Also in Woodstock is the Raptor Center of the Vermont Institute of Natural Science. Over 20 species of raptors (birds that eat other animals), all found injured in the wild, now flourish on this nature preserve. Among them are a bald eagle and a peregrine falcon.

Traveling west to Proctor, don't miss the Vermont Marble Exhibit. Learn more about one of Vermont's most valuable natural resources, and watch a marble sculptor create a piece of art from a piece of stone.

Southern Vermont

Near Manchester, Bromley Mountain is a center of outdoor activity. In winter, families can go skiing, snowboarding, ice skating, or snowmobiling. Even without snow, there's still lots to do. At Bromley's Thrill Zone, try zooming down the Alpine slide, parabouncing on a huge trampoline, or climbing the 24-foot (7-m) rock wall.

Next, take a farm tour at the Adams Farm in Wilmington. The livestock barn has all kinds of animals for petting, including horses, calves, goats, sheep, llamas, and pigs. Try your hand at milking a goat. You can also take a hayride or a sleigh ride to get a good view of the Vermont countryside.

Like a glacier moving over land, we've only scratched the surface of all things there are to do and see in Vermont. If you visit, make like a glacier and move slowly, so that you don't miss a thing.

VERMONT ALMANAC

Statehood date and number: March 4, 1791, the 14th state

State seal: A circle bordered on  the top and bottom by wavy lines indicating sky and water, it features sheaves of wheat, a cow, a pine tree, and hills and forests. It was originally designed by Ira Allen, Ethan Allen's brother. Adopted 1937.

State flag: The Vermont state coat of arms on a blue field. Adopted 1919.

Geographic center: In Washington County, east of Roxbury

Total area/rank: 9,614 square miles (24,901 sq km)/45th

Borders: Massachusetts, New Hampshire, New York, and Quebec, Canada

Latitude and longitude: Vermont is located approximately between 42° 44' and 45° 01' N and 71° 33' and 73° 26' W.

Highest/lowest elevation: Mount Mansfield, 4,380 feet (1,336 m)/Lake Champlain, 95 feet (29 m)

Hottest/coldest temperature: 105°F (41°C) on July 4, 1911 in Vernon/−50°F (−46°C) on December 30, 1933 in Bloomfield

Land area/rank: 9,250 square miles (23,956 sq km)/43rd

Inland water area/rank: 365 square miles (945 sq km)/40th

Population (2000 census)/rank: 608,827/49th

Population of major cities:

Burlington: 38,889

Essex: 18,626

Rutland: 17,292

Colchester: 16,986

S. Burlington: 15,814

Bennington: 15,737

Origin of state name: From the French words *les monts verts*, which means "green mountains." In 1777, Dr. Thomas Young suggested combining *vert* and *mont* into Vermont.

State capital: Montpelier, 1805

Counties: 14

State government: 30 senators, 150 representatives

Major rivers/lakes: Otter Creek, Missisquoi River, Lamoille River, Winooski River/Lake Champlain, Lake Memphremagog, Lake Bomoseen

Farm products: Dairy products, apples, maple syrup

Livestock: Cattle, sheep, hogs

Manufactured products: Machine tools, furniture, computer components

Mining products: Granite, talc, marble

Animal: Morgan horse

Bird: Hermit thrush

Butterfly: Monarch butterfly

Coldwater fish: Brook trout

Flower: Red clover

Gem: Grossular garnet

Insect: Honeybee

Mineral: Talc

Motto: Freedom and Unity

Nickname: The Green Mountain State

Rocks: Marble, granite, slate

Song: "These Green Mountains," words and music by Diane Martin. Adopted 2000.

Tree: Sugar maple

Warmwater fish: Walleye pike

TIMELINE

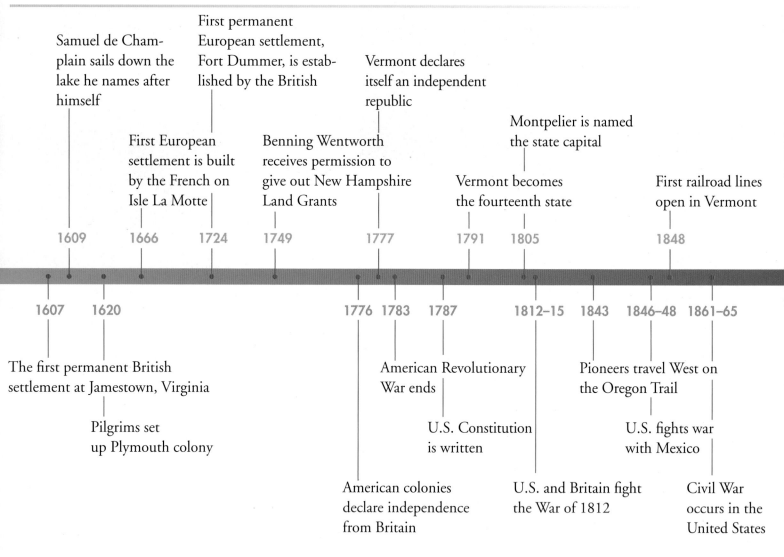

Samuel de Champlain sails down the lake he names after himself

First permanent European settlement, Fort Dummer, is established by the British

Vermont declares itself an independent republic

Montpelier is named the state capital

First European settlement is built by the French on Isle La Motte

Benning Wentworth receives permission to give out New Hampshire Land Grants

Vermont becomes the fourteenth state

First railroad lines open in Vermont

1609   1666   1724   1749   1777   1791   1805   1848

1607   1620   1776   1783   1787   1812–15   1843   1846–48   1861–65

The first permanent British settlement at Jamestown, Virginia

Pilgrims set up Plymouth colony

American Revolutionary War ends

Pioneers travel West on the Oregon Trail

U.S. Constitution is written

U.S. fights war with Mexico

American colonies declare independence from Britain

U.S. and Britain fight the War of 1812

Civil War occurs in the United States

UNITED STATES HISTORY

Madeleine M. Kunin becomes Vermont's first female governor

Vermont native Chester A. Arthur becomes 21st U.S. president

Billy Kidd of Stowe wins silver and bronze medals for slalom and Alpine skiing in 1964 Olympics

Middlebury College is honored by the U.S. Postal Service with its own postcard

Vermonter Calvin Coolidge becomes 30th U.S. president

The Environmental Control Law is passed

| 1881 | 1923 | 1964 | 1970 | 1985 | 2000 |

| 1917–18 | 1929 | 1941–45 | 1950–53 | 1964 | 1965–73 | 1969 | 1991 | 1995 |

U.S. takes part in World War I

U.S. fights in World War II

Civil rights laws passed in the U.S.

U.S. and other nations fight in Persian Gulf War

U.S. fights in the Vietnam War

The stock market crashes and U.S. enters the Great Depression

U.S. fights in the Korean War

Neil Armstrong and Edwin Aldrin land on the moon

U.S. space shuttle docks with Russian space station

GALLERY OF FAMOUS VERMONTERS

Chester A. Arthur
(1829–1886)
Succeeded to the presidency following the death of President James A. Garfield. Arthur was the 21st president of the United States. Born in Fairfield.

Kelly Clark
(1983–)
Gold-medal winner in the women's halfpipe competition (snowboarding) at the 2002 Winter Olympics. Lives in West Dover.

Calvin Coolidge
(1872–1933)
Succeeded to the presidency following the death of Warren G. Harding. Served from 1923 to 1929. He was the 30th president of the United States. Born in Plymouth.

Admiral George Dewey
(1837–1917)
A national hero for his role in the Spanish American War, when his fleet defeated Spanish forces in Manila Bay. Born in Montpelier.

Robert Frost
(1874–1963)
World-renowned poet and winner of four Pulitzer Prizes. Frost was poet laureate of Vermont. He often wrote of the beauty of nature and the landscape of New England.

John LeClair
(1969–)
Hockey player. Born in St. Albans, he played first for the Montreal Canadiens and later for the Philadelphia Flyers.

Norman Rockwell
(1894–1978)
A well-known artist who is best known for his paintings of small-town life. He lived in Arlington and often used his neighbors as models for his work.

Patty Sheehan
(1956–)
Professional golfer. Youngest person to be honored as a member of the Ladies' Professional Golf Association Hall of Fame. Born in Middlebury.

GLOSSARY

agriculture: farming

assassinated: killed, usually for political or religious reasons

erosion: the gradual wearing away of land by water, wind, or ice

fossil: the hardened remains of an animal or plant from times long ago

foundation: the basis, or establishment, of an institution

glacier: a large, slow-moving mass of ice

immigrant: a person who comes to a foreign country to live permanently

inhabitants: residents, people or animals, who live in a certain place

nomad: someone who moves from place to place

pollute: to make dirty or contaminate

portico: a porch or covered walkway

prospered: thrived

quaint: pleasingly old-fashioned

quarry: place where stone is dug, cut, or blasted out

receding: withdrawing, moving away from

resumed: continued

skirmish: a short fight

tourism: the business of serving people who are traveling or vacationing

tyrannical: acting like a strict or severe power figure

FOR MORE INFORMATION

Web sites

Welcome to the State of Vermont
http://vermont.gov
The official homepage of the state of Vermont.

Vermont Explorer
http://www.1-800-vermont.com/
The official site of the Vermont Department of Tourism and Marketing.

Books

Aronson, Virginia. *Ethan Allen, Revolutionary Hero.* Broomall, PA: Chelsea House Publishing, 2000.

January, Brendan. *The Lincoln-Douglas Debates (Cornerstones of Freedom).* Danbury, CT: Children's Press, 1998.

Joseph, Paul. *Calvin Coolidge.* Edina, MN: Abdo & Daughters, 2000.

Addresses

Vermont Department of Tourism and Marketing
National Life Bldg.,
6th Floor, Drawer 20
Montpelier, VT 05620-0501

Vermont Chamber of Commerce
PO Box 37
Montpelier, VT 05601

Governor of Vermont
109 State Street, Pavilion
Montpelier, VT 05609-0101

INDEX

MEET THE AUTHOR

Jan M. Czech is a former middle school English teacher and the author of three published picture books, *An American Face*, *The Garden Angel*, and *The Coffee Can Kid*. She also writes for a daily newspaper and has more than 300 published articles on everything from lighthouses to chimpanzees. Czech is an instructor for The Institute of Children's Literature and a member of the Society of Children's Book Writers and Illustrators.

She lives in Western New York with her husband, daughter, golden retriever, and two cats. She has visited Vermont many times.

Photographs © 2009: AP Images: 53 (Toby Talbot), 74 right; Bridgeman Art Library International Ltd., London/New York: 33 (CH89269, Covered Bridge at West Arlington, VT, (oil on masonite), Sloane, Eric Private Collection/Christie's Images), 36 bottom (HTD82767, Abraham Lincoln and Stephen A. Douglas debating at Charleston, IL on 18th September 1858, Root, Robert Marshall, State Historical Library of Illinois, Chicago, IL); Brown Brothers: 41; Corbis Images: 74 top left (Bettmann), 64 (Richard T. Nowitz), 3 right, 65, 67 (Phil Schermeister), 42 (UPI); Dembinsky Photo Assoc./Anthony Mercieca: 71 left; Getty Images: 37 top (Archive Photos), 30 (Hulton Archive); ImageState/Andre Jenny: 10, 50, 56; Jeb Wallace-Brodeur: 4, 20; Kindra Clineff: 55, 70 right, 71 bottom right; Library of Congress/Louis L. McAllister: 39; MapQuest.com, Inc.: 70 bottom left; New York State Museum, Albany, NY: 36 top; North Wind Picture Archives: 23, 24, 27, 29, 31, 32, 34, 38; Courtesy of the family of Perry Merrill: 12; Photo Researchers, NY: 3 left (David R. Frazier), 15 (Paul J. Fusco), 9 (Robert A. Isaacs), 19 (S.R. Maglione), 11 (Peter Miller); Robertstock.com/H. Abernathy: 8; Sandy Macys Photography: 16, 21, 44, 46; Stock Montage, Inc.: 26, 40 bottom; Superstock, Inc.: cover, 28, 45, 47 background; Terry Donnelly: 7; The Image Works: 62 (Alden Pellett), 59, 63 (Steven Rubin); Tom Till Photography, Inc.: 18; Unicorn Stock Photos/Andre Jenny: 14; Vermont Historical Society: 37 bottom (Houghton Collection), 40 top, 74 bottom left; Vermont Secretary of State: 70 top left; Visuals Unlimited: 71 top right (Wally Eberhart), 52 (Jeff Greenberg).